TO HAVE AND TO HOLED

RAISED AND GLAZED COZY MYSTERIES, BOOK
39

EMMA AINSLEY

SUMMER PRESCOTT BOOKS PUBLISHING

ONE

"I just can't get over how beautiful it is out here this time of year," Suzan Logan declared. She was seated in front of Maggie Mission, her future mother-in-law, as they rode around on the farm where Suzan's wedding to Maggie's son Bradley was set to take place in just under two weeks.

"It is beautiful," Maggie said. She glanced at Ruby Cobb, her best friend, business partner, and owner of the land on which they were now traveling and smiled. "There's nothing like the countryside in the Ozarks in the fall."

"Just watch out for the cow pies." Ruby chuckled from her seat behind the wheel of a small all-terrain vehicle. Maggie was seated in the back next to her grandson, Wyatt, with Suzan holding on to her small daughter, Chloe, in the front.

"What are cow pies?" Chloe asked her mother. Suzan glanced nervously back at Maggie, desperate for a lifeline.

"Cow pies are what we call it when cows go to the bathroom," Maggie said quickly.

"You are so good at thinking on your feet when it comes to kids' questions," Suzan said.

"I think that comes with years of experience," Maggie said, laughing off the compliment. "Besides, I've had a lot of time with Wyatt as well," she said, glancing down at her small grandson. "He has had plenty of questions about life out here on Aunt Ruby's farm."

"I can't thank you enough for letting us hold the wedding here," Suzan said, beaming at Ruby.

"It's been my pleasure." Ruby smiled. "This isn't the first wedding we've had out here, after all. It's become something of a tradition for our extended family."

"Speaking of family," Maggie said. "When are your parents set to arrive?"

"Well, my mother and stepfather are supposed to be here at the end of the week," Suzan said. "My father and his wife will be here at the beginning of the week."

"Forgive me for asking," Ruby said. "But what are their names again? I can't keep everyone straight."

"It's okay," Suzan said. "There are a lot of people to keep track of, especially since most of my aunts and uncles plan to attend the wedding as well. Anne is my mother and Lester is my stepfather. They will be here late Thursday or early Friday."

"And they're staying at the Dogwood House," Maggie interrupted.

"Yes, they have rooms set up there," Suzan said. "They were especially excited to book the bed and breakfast when they found out how it fits into your family's history. The fact that it belonged to your late aunt is quite the matter of pride for Bradley."

"That's really sweet," Ruby said.

"Anyway, my dad's name is Bill. His wife's name is Sandra," Suzan continued. Maggie noted how her mood soured when she mentioned her father's name.

"Where are your father and his wife staying?" Ruby asked.

"I'm not sure yet," Suzan said. "I wouldn't be surprised if they tried to book a room at the Dogwood House just because that's where Mom and Lester are going."

"It sounds like there's a bit of strife between your mother and father," Maggie said. She had no desire to pry, but she wanted to be prepared in case there were issues that came up during the wedding preparations.

"More like between my stepmother and everyone else," Suzan said. She gazed out at the tree line in the distance. "Honestly, my dad and my mom get along just fine. Dad and Lester get along well, too."

"Forgive me for asking," Ruby said. "But who is walking you down the aisle?"

"Both Dad and Lester are walking me down the aisle," Suzan said.

"That's really amazing," Maggie said. "I'm sure there are other families who could take a lesson from yours."

"My dad was the one who suggested it," Suzan said. "Since I was so little when my parents got divorced, Lester has been there for as long as I can remember. My dad said that it would be a crime not to include him on my wedding day."

"This is your second wedding," Maggie said carefully. "How did things go the first time?"

"The first time my stepmother made a mess of things," Suzan said. "She went around playing the part of the bridezilla instead of me." She chuckled and shook her head.

"Hopefully she's had some time to mature since then," Maggie said.

"If a woman in her sixties can mature," Suzan said ruefully. "My stepmother is quite a few years older than my own mother, which is part of the problem."

"Is your stepmother jealous of your mother?" Ruby asked.

"My stepmother has to be the center of attention regardless of where she's at," Suzan said.

"Well, we certainly have the best view for a wedding," Maggie said, determined to change the subject. The last thing she wanted was for her young grandson or Suzan's little daughter to overhear their conversation and repeat it at the wrong time.

"You are right about that." Suzan smiled. "I can't think of a more beautiful place to become Bradley's wife."

"And my new mom." Wyatt giggled. Maggie and Ruby began to chuckle as well. Suzan reached back and squeezed the little boy's hand.

When they returned to Ruby's farmhouse to join Brett, Maggie's husband, and Bradley, the mood was light. Ruby had invited both of the couples out for an early dinner. Unlike most Sunday afternoons, the guest list stopped with just Maggie and her family. Typically, other members of the staff at Dogwood Donuts would have been invited, but today was reserved for wedding talk.

While the women and the children had been on a ride over the countryside, Brett and Bradley had taken the time to lay out the seating arrangement in the grand barn on the hill overlooking the farmhouse. It was the suggestion of Alexandra, Suzan and Bradley's wedding planner, to mark exactly where they wanted things set up.

Conversation during dinner turned to the planned honeymoon. Suzan explained how her sister Julie intended to take both children for the week while Bradley and herself flew to Jamaica. Suzan bubbled with excitement over her new job, a position she planned to take after returning from Jamaica.

"So, you'll no longer be at the hospital in Joplin, then?" Ruby asked as she stood and cleared the table.

"Oh, no," Suzan said. "I don't want to be that far away from Hunter Springs."

"Do you remember the old outpost clinic, Mom?" Bradley asked. "It's north of Dogwood Mountain a bit, but about fifteen minutes away from our house."

"I remember the old clinic," Maggie said. After having grown up in Dogwood Mountain, Missouri, and moving away, Maggie returned home when her aunt Marjorie Getz passed away, leaving her small cottage home and the donut shop to Maggie in her will. After her return home, she reconnected with her high school crush, Brett Mission, then chief of the Dogwood Mountain Police Department. Since then, Brett had served as County Sheriff, then retired to run a third location for the donut shop. Bradley ran his own store in Hunter Springs.

"I remember it, too," Brett said. "It seems like a lot of rural people utilized the services there."

"Yes, they did for many years," Suzan said. "Anyway, there was a job opening there and I jumped on it."

"Did the clinic just reopen?" Maggie asked.

"Yes, with a new staff and everything," Suzan said.

"Suzan will be in charge." Bradley beamed.

"You will be? That's incredible," Ruby said.

"I hope so," Suzan said, smiling nervously. "It will be my first job as a new nurse practitioner. I've been studying for my degree for years, ever since leaving nursing school as a registered nurse. And now that I have my credentials, I can run the clinic. Under a doctor's supervision, of course."

"What a gift to the area," Brett said. "A lot of those people have a hard time making it into Hunter Springs, let alone all the way to Joplin."

"That's what they said at my interview. They're hoping I can come in and provide services, even emergency first aid as needed, to save those people a trip to the hospital."

"I'm very proud of my future wife," Bradley said. "If you can't tell already."

"Oh, we can tell," Brett said, punching his stepson lightly in the arm.

TWO

Maggie woke up late Monday morning, then scampered to get ready for work. The short distance from her house to the donut shop, less than a block, made it easier for her to make up for lost time. When she arrived, she was surprised to see Ruby's pickup truck already parked in the alley behind the building.

"Late night?" Ruby teased when Maggie walked in.

"How could you tell?" Maggie asked.

"Maybe because you still have toothpaste on your mouth." Ruby laughed, indicating the right side of Maggie's face.

"Oh, you've got to be kidding," Maggie said. She hung up her jacket and hurried to the employee restroom located in the back of the kitchen. "You wouldn't believe how late we were up talking to Lester and Anne last night."

"Suzan's mother and stepfather? How did that go?"

"Amazing," Maggie said, poking her head out of the opened door to the bathroom. "Anne is incredible. Lester and Brett share a lot of common interests. I can't believe how nice they are. But, knowing Suzan as we do now, I see where she gets it."

"Do you have plans to meet her father and step-mother?" Ruby asked.

"None yet," Maggie said. "I found out they're staying at the motel, so I planned to pop in on them this afternoon. I figured I could bring them a basket of treats and some coffee. We both know the coffee at the Dogwood Mountain Motel is not the best."

"That will make a good impression," Ruby said. "Do you want some company?"

"Sure," Maggie said with a smile. She flipped off the light in the bathroom and headed toward her office, grabbing a clean apron from a hook outside of the storeroom. "If you're up for it, I'm sure they would like to meet you as well."

"Are we doing any sort of special next week?" Ruby asked. "To celebrate the wedding?"

"I just haven't had time to discover a new recipe," Maggie said. She dropped her shoulders and shook her head. "I know I should have been on it already, but this wedding has me running around chasing my own tail."

"Why don't you leave that to me?" Ruby suggested. "I've been playing around with flavors again."

"It's hard to come up with something new sometimes," Maggie said. "We've had apple cider doughnuts, pumpkin spice doughnuts, just about everything else under the sun."

"Yes, that's true," Ruby nodded. "But we haven't had an apple streusel donut just yet."

"Apple streusel? I'm not sure what that would look like," Maggie said.

"Think of it as part apple fritter, part coffee cake," Ruby said. "I'll bring you a sample in the morning. You can judge for yourself."

"You know what?" Maggie said, holding her hands up. "You just create some magic like you always do and if you want to put it on the menu, go for it. You have my full support."

"Are you sure?" Ruby asked.

"The last time I checked, we were co-owners of this business. Of course, it's fine if you add something to the menu without consulting me first. In fact, it will take quite a load off my back."

"I'll be in early tomorrow morning to make the first round," Ruby said. "We'll see how they sell."

"Good morning, mother of the groom," Naomi Gardner, one of Maggie's closest friends and employee, crooned when she walked through the back door just before opening.

"Mother of the groom is right," Maggie said, rolling her eyes. "These wedding plans have me chasing myself in circles. I don't even feel like myself right now."

"I remember feeling the same way when I got married," Myra Sawyer-Macklin, wife of Brooks Macklin and the current chief of police, said.

"It will all be over soon enough," Ruby said. "By the way, the caterer was in touch with me this morning. Everything is set for the wedding."

"How many people are you expecting?" Myra asked.

"Three hundred," Maggie said, nodding. "Those kids expect three hundred people to fit inside that barn."

"Fitting them inside the barn isn't the issue," Ruby said. "It's the parking I worry about."

"I hope no one tears up your pasture," Naomi said.

"Oh, we have a contingency plan in place for that." Maggie smiled.

"Contingency plan," Myra repeated. "What are you going to do, put up concrete blocks?"

"More like big stumps of an oak tree," Ruby said. "I had to cut down a few trees last year. The stumps are as wide as a dinner table. And now they're hard as rocks since they've been sitting out in the weather. I dare anyone to try to drive over that."

"What exactly is the theme for the menu?" Naomi asked. "I forgot to ask Bradley when I was in Hunter Springs last week."

"I'm not sure Bradley remembers himself," Maggie joked. "But they want a trip around the world."

"Which means finger foods and appetizers from various countries," Ruby said. "But the wedding cake is traditional."

"As long as they've got it handled," Myra said. "That's all that really matters."

"I agree with you there," Maggie said. "I'm so glad they hired a wedding planner."

Maggie glanced at the clock and hurried back to her place at the baker's table. She still had several batches of cinnamon rolls to prepare, and the clock was ticking. Myra and Naomi took over as soon as the front doors opened, while Maggie remained in the kitchen with Ruby, chatting lightly about the upcoming nuptials.

Around nine, business slowed down for a bit. Maggie announced her intention to enjoy a cinnamon roll and a cup of coffee out front in her usual booth on the far side of the counter. She invited Ruby to join her, but she shrugged her off. "I want to put out some samples of those apple streusel donuts soon," she explained.

"Suit yourself," Maggie said. "By the way, I expect a full-sized sample for myself."

"Count on it," Ruby said, waving her off with a grin. Maggie decided to treat herself to her husband's favorite beverage, a cinnamon latte, then get off her feet for at least thirty minutes. She was surprised to see Orson Hawley, former employee and dear friend, make his appearance when she made her way to the booth.

"Finally taking a break, are you?" Orson mumbled. He removed his coat and hung it up on a chair pushed up to the Old Timer's table, his favorite spot. He then made his way behind the counter and poured himself a cup of coffee, and then opened the display case and took his time choosing a donut.

Maggie heard the door chime and felt a gust of cold wind, but she kept her back turned to the front of the donut shop. Instead, she blew on the surface of her cinnamon latte and carefully sipped the hot liquid.

"Are you Bradley's father?" a shrill voice demanded, catching Maggie by surprise. She turned around in her seat. A large woman with bleach blonde hair pounded her fist on the front counter. "Hey. I'm talking to you. Are you Bradley's father?"

"Oh, I'm sorry," Orson said, turning around slowly. "I don't tend to respond to people who sound like an off-key banshee."

"Just answer my question," the woman said. "I want to speak to Bradley Sharpe's parents. Right now."

"Well, you've come to the wrong place for that," Orson said.

"What do you mean?" the woman demanded. "I thought his mother owned this place."

"I'm not saying she doesn't," Orson said. "What I am saying is you're not going to get a reaction from anyone while you're still yelling at me. Why don't you calm down and tell me what you need."

"Are you his father or not?" the woman repeated.

"He is not," Maggie said, standing up abruptly. "But I am his mother, and I would appreciate it if you could lower your voice. You're disturbing my customers."

"Well, they should be disturbed," the woman continued. "I demand to know what is going on with this wedding cake fiasco."

"Is there a problem?" Ruby asked, emerging from the back.

"I don't know," the woman said. "You tell me. Why is a donut shop making my daughter's wedding cake?"

"Who are you exactly?" Maggie said.

"I happen to be Sandra Logan. I am the mother of the bride."

"Oh, great," Orson quipped on his way back to his table.

Maggie abandoned her cinnamon roll and latte at her table and made her way behind the counter. She stood just feet from Sandra. "I presume you are Suzan's stepmother, married to her father, Bill."

"That is not for you to determine," Sandra said. "I want to know which of you clowns is planning to ruin my daughter's wedding by making a wedding cake out of donuts?"

"No one is making their wedding cake out of donuts," Ruby said. "In fact, we're not making the wedding cake."

"That's not the way I heard it," Sandra said. She stepped away from the counter, then rushed to the end, and stepped behind it. Before Maggie could stop her, she had made her way to the swinging door between the dining area in the kitchen.

"Hey, you can't go back there," Maggie said.

"I sure as heck can," Sandra said. "If I'm paying for all of this, I demand to see the kitchen where everything will be made."

Ruby stepped in front of the woman and blocked her entrance. "You are not allowed back here," she said. "For one thing, it is a public health violation. For another, you've already been told that we aren't the ones doing the cake or anything for the wedding."

"I want to talk to Bradley," Sandra said. "And I mean now. Right now."

"My son isn't here," Maggie said, dumbfounded at the woman's attitude. "He's in Hunter Springs."

"I thought he had a job," Sandra said. "Are you telling me my Suzan is about to marry some unemployed bum?"

"Now you've done it," Orson called over his coffee mug from the Old Timer's table. "Let her have it, Maggie."

"For one thing," Maggie said, counting to ten in her head to remain calm. "My son is no bum. He is employed at a donut shop, but it's the location in Hunter Springs, which he runs himself."

"He's not here, then," Sandra said. "Is that what you're telling me?"

"No, he is not," Maggie said. "Why don't you call Suzan and make arrangements to meet with the two of them for dinner?"

"Why don't you get out of my way?" Sandra said to Ruby, who was still standing in front of her.

"Because you're not going in this kitchen," Ruby said. "At this point, you'll be lucky to step foot on my property on the day of the wedding."

"Who are you?" Sandra sneered.

"As I said, I'm the owner of the property where your stepdaughter plans to tie the knot."

"That's right," Sandra said, wrinkling her nose. "They chose to get married in a barn, of all places. What kind of potent place is this?"

"I think it's time for you to go," Maggie said.

"Lady, I'm not going anywhere," Sandra said. "And you better play nice if you expect to have anything to do with little Chloe and any of the other babies that come along."

"I already have a pretty good relationship with little Chloe, thank you very much," Maggie snapped.

"That's enough," Ruby said, taking a step toward the woman.

"Hey, stop pushing me," Sandra complained. Ruby continued to walk her out from behind the counter.

"I think maybe you should go back to your motel room and take a nap or something," Ruby said. "You need a reset. Maybe it's all the time traveling to get here, but you're acting like an unreasonable jerk."

"What did you just call me?" Sandra demanded.

"She said you're a jerk," Orson called from his table.

"Orson," Maggie said, giving him a stern look.

"What? The woman must be hard of hearing," Orson said.

"How dare you?" Sandra spun around and confronted Orson.

"Oh, I dare rather easily, thank you," Orson said, grinning.

"Sandra, there you are," a man said, bursting through the front door. "I've been looking for you everywhere."

"Please tell me you are Suzan's father," Maggie said.

"I am," the man said. "The name is Bill Logan. And you are?"

"The rudest woman on planet earth," Sandra cut in.

"My name is Maggie Mission," Maggie said. "Bradley is my son."

Bill blanched and gripped the back of a chair. "Oh, I am so sorry," he said. "Sandra, let's go and leave these people alone."

"Not until I see that kitchen," Sandra said, lunging toward the counter again. Ruby was too quick for her, though. She blocked the entrance to the back.

"Are you making trouble here, Sandra?" Bill asked. "It's bad enough you had to move our accommodations to the same place Anne and Lester are staying."

"Wow. This just gets better and better." Orson chuckled.

"Who is that?" Bill asked, turning toward the Old Timer's table.

"Just some loudmouth old man," Sandra said. "He acts like he's got some sort of say in what goes on in this place."

"That's because I do, lady," Orson said. "If this is your wife, dear sir, you have my sympathies."

"What did you just say?" Sandra shouted.

"That's enough of this," Bill said. He stood, suddenly finding a backbone, then took his wife by the arm and led her through the front door.

"Well, that went well," Orson said after Sandra and Bill Logan had left the donut shop. "This wedding is off to a great start already."

THREE

Maggie heard nothing more from Bill or Sandra for the remainder of the workday. As soon as she returned home from work that afternoon, she filled Brett in on the incident at the donut shop.

"This is going to be one heck of a wedding to get through," Brett said.

"Just be glad you were over at the Jefferson Street location instead of the main location today," Maggie said. She plopped down on the couch in her most comfortable pair of sweats and closed her eyes.

"What was up with Orson today?" Brett chuckled. "It sounds like he was really instigating things."

"I didn't know whether to thank him or shout at him for his behavior while Sandra was there," Maggie said. She opened her eyes and gazed at her husband. "Although, there was nothing he said that was wrong."

"Leave it to Orson to tell the truth," Brett said. "No matter how crass it is."

"I'm just dreading the phone call with Bradley after what happened," Maggie said. "I hope he doesn't blame me for the way we reacted."

"After what Suzan said about her stepmother, I hardly think that's going to be an issue."

"Well," Maggie said, glancing at the screen of her cell phone which had just begun to ring. "I suppose we'll find out soon enough. Here's Suzan calling me now."

"Good luck," Brett said. "I'll be in the kitchen making dinner." He got up and left Maggie alone in the living room to answer her phone.

"Hello," Maggie said calmly.

"Oh, Maggie," Suzan said on the other end, then dissolved into a fit of sobs. "I am so, so sorry for what happened today."

"Calm down, sweetheart," Maggie said. "If you're referring to your stepmother's visit to the donut shop, you have nothing to apologize for."

"I feel like this is my responsibility," Suzan said. "I should have been there when she showed up."

"The last time I checked, you have other things to worry about," Maggie said. "You don't have time to babysit your stepmother."

"I can't believe how demanding she was," Suzan said.

"How did you know anything about it?" Maggie asked. She was genuinely curious. She had not said a word to her son.

"My dad told me," Suzan said. "I called Myra and made her fill in the blanks."

"You and Myra have become pretty good friends," Maggie said. She was hoping she might redirect the conversation somewhere else. "I think that's wonderful."

"Myra has become my best friend lately," Suzan said. "She told me how awful Sandra was; how Ruby had to block her from going into the kitchen."

"It was quite the scene," Maggie said. "Your dad came in and made her leave with him. No harm was done."

"Plenty of harm was done," Suzan said, followed by a fresh round of sobs.

"Suzan, dear," Maggie said softly. "Don't let this ruin your excitement about the wedding. You let other people work out their own issues. You just focus on yourself, Bradley, and the kids. In fact, don't you worry one bit about Sandra."

"I'm afraid it may not be that easy," Suzan said, sniffing loudly. "Once she's in a tear like this, it's hard to control her. She's going to ruin the wedding."

"Oh, no she won't," Maggie said, doing her best to reassure her future daughter-in-law. "There are enough of us around that will intercept her on the day of your wedding. I can promise you that. Brett, Ruby, Naomi, Myra, and I, even Orson, have no problem running interference at the wedding or the reception."

"I appreciate that, Maggie," Suzan said. "I really do. But I'm afraid Sandra is an expert at getting her digs in wherever she wants to."

"Maybe you should have a talk with your dad," Maggie suggested. "I hate to be this way, but it might be worth considering uninviting her to the wedding if you have concerns."

"I never invited her in the first place," Suzan said. "I've had a conversation with my father about it and everything. I told him I wanted him and Lester to walk me down the aisle, but that I didn't want Sandra there. Dad told me he would take care of it, but obviously, that didn't help."

"Like I said," Maggie repeated. "Just concentrate on the wedding. Leave the rest of it up to us. Remember, there will be at least two law enforcement officers in attendance. Well, one retired law enforcement officer, but the effect will be the same. I have a feeling Brooks won't mind escorting your stepmother off the property if things get too bad."

"I'd love nothing more than to see her leaving my reception in the back of a police car with the sirens blaring," Suzan said, laughing lightly. "I know that's awful to say."

"After seeing your stepmother in action this morning," Maggie said. "I don't think there's a thing wrong with how you feel." They ended their phone call and Maggie rested her head on the back of the couch.

"How did that go?" Brett asked, poking his head into the living room from the kitchen.

"She was crying so hard," Maggie said, sitting forward and shaking her head. "She feels so bad, and I feel so bad for her. That woman is simply awful."

"I heard you threaten her with a ride in a police car," Brett said. "I know we can make that happen."

"I hope it's enough just to issue the threat," Maggie said. She stood and joined Brett in the kitchen. "Looks like you're making your world-famous spaghetti tonight."

"Anything for you, my dear," he said, then bumped his hip into hers, knocking her across the kitchen.

"You'd better not start with me," Maggie said, hiding her smile. "I'm capable of anything after the day I've had."

FOUR

An hour later, they stood side by side washing up the few dishes in the sink after dinner. Brett regaled Maggie with a few tales of his own from work, then suddenly stopped talking. "You can't get the wedding off your mind, can you?"

"Oh, I'm sorry," Maggie said. "I wasn't trying to ignore you, but I'm worried about Bradley and Suzan."

"They're going to work things out," Brett reassured her. "That's what adults do. And both have been adults for a little while. They are parents, after all. They're not teenagers running off to elope."

"I know, and I know that Bradley was in the Navy and now he runs a successful business. I know that they've both raised their children by themselves, and I also know that Suzan is so capable, she completed her studies as a nurse practitioner at quite a young age. Even so, I can't help but feel a little maternal toward them as a whole."

"Is that what we call it? Because I think I'm feeling maternal, too." Brett grinned. "I would have been so tempted to put that woman in handcuffs and shove her out the door."

"I think that's maybe what she needs," Maggie said. She tossed the towel onto the counter and headed to the restroom.

"There's someone at the door," Brett called down the hall after her. "I'll get it."

Maggie took an extra moment at the bathroom sink to wash her hands. Whoever it was, aside from her own child and his fiancée, she willed them away. Her patience had been stretched thin. She wanted nothing more than to climb into bed and pull the covers over her head.

But when she emerged from the hallway, she was surprised to see Anne and Lester standing in the kitchen. "I'm so sorry for bothering you," Anne said as Maggie entered the kitchen.

"It's no problem," Maggie said with a smile. "Is something wrong?"

"I'm afraid we have some terrible news," Anne said. She opened her mouth to speak again, but put her hand over her mouth and began to cry.

Lester rested his arms on his wife's shoulders and pulled her in tight. "This is difficult for Anne to talk about," he said. "But I'm afraid that the wedding planner, Alexandra, has suddenly quit, leaving us in quite a lurch."

"She quit? Why would she do that?" Brett asked. "That seems terribly unprofessional."

"What happened?" Maggie asked. She could feel her pulse pounding against her temples. Her throat suddenly got very dry. She had a sinking feeling that she already knew the answer to her question.

"Sandra happened," Lester said. It was the first time she had seen him display any sort of negative opinion of his stepdaughter's other family members.

"Why don't we all have a seat at the table?" Brett suggested. Lester pulled a chair out for Anne and carefully led her onto it. Brett nodded at Maggie, then removed four wine glasses from the cabinet next to the sink and grabbed an unopened bottle of sweet red wine.

"Thank you," Lester said when he accepted a glass for himself and for his wife. "I understand you had quite the run in with Sandra this morning at your donut shop."

"That's one way to put it," Maggie said.

"After she left with Bill," Lester continued. "She convinced him that she was going to go back to the bed and breakfast and take a nap. Only, she had other plans."

"They shouldn't have been staying at the bed and breakfast in the first place," Anne managed to say between tears.

"I think that's a given," Brett said.

"Anyway, Sandra got up and took their car and headed across town," Lester explained. "She wound up at Alexandra's office in Hunter Springs. Really, it was Alexandra's home since she works out of there.

Anyway, Sandra beat on her front door until she opened it, and then pushed her way inside and gave her a piece of her mind. She demanded to see the plans for the wedding."

"You're kidding," Maggie said in disbelief. "She barged into that poor woman's home?"

"She destroyed it." Anne sobbed. "When Sandra couldn't get her way, she started taking paintings off the wall and pushing over furniture."

"I hope Alexandra called the police." Brett gasped. "She should be sitting in jail right now for that behavior."

"When Bill realized what happened, he borrowed a car from Ms. LeClair, at the bed and breakfast," Lester said.

"Gretchen is quite a good friend of ours," Maggie said, nodding and understanding.

"Anyway, by the time Bill got there, Alexandra was in tears on the floor. He talked her out of filing formal charges," Lester said. "But Alexandra quit on the spot. She won't be returning any deposits or anything else."

"I can't say I blame her," Brett said.

"But now what are they going to do?" Anne said. Her eyes were red and swollen from crying. "Suzan wants this wedding to be perfect. Now what will happen?"

"For one thing," Maggie said. "The wedding venue never required a deposit in the first place. Ruby is my best friend and while she isn't biologically related to my son, she's as close as if she were. He calls her Aunt Ruby, after all. The wedding venue will not be changed."

"That's reassuring," Anne said. "But what about everything else? Alexandra was the one handling the caterer and everything from the flowers to the wedding cake."

"I'm sure we can manage that," Brett said.

"I think he's right," Lester said to his wife. "I'm sure we can arrange to have the food delivered and handle organizing the wedding cake."

"As long as that horrid woman stays away from the caterer," Anne said.

"Even if she doesn't," Maggie said. "It wouldn't be the first time we've pulled together a wedding at the last moment. Ruby is a trained executive chef, and she's also the author of several bestselling cookbooks. She has friends who will come together at a moment's notice if needed."

"Are you sure?" Anne said, her eyes searching Maggie's face.

"Absolutely positive," Maggie said. She reached across the table and patted Anne's hand. "It might be time for all of us to get together and have an intervention with this woman."

"What do you mean?" Lester said.

"I mean, it might be time for the rest of us to confront Sandra and tell her the way things are going to go," Maggie said. She felt her anger begin to rise up in her throat. "I never ever thought I would say this, but maybe the four of us need to go over there and have a talk with her."

"Count me in," Ruby said, standing in the back door frame. "I knocked before I let myself in."

"Oh, sorry I didn't hear," Maggie said. "I'm a little distracted."

"Lester, Anne," Brett said. "Meet Ruby Cobb."

"Oh, you must be Aunt Ruby." Anne laughed and sprung up from her chair to cross the kitchen floor. She wrapped Ruby in a bear hug and squeezed her tightly. "Thank you for everything you've done for our children."

"Trust me," Ruby said. "It has been my pleasure. I just wish there wasn't so much else going on for these poor kids."

"You mean Sandra, I assume?" Anne frowned.

"She's the reason the wedding planner just up and quit," Maggie said, filling Ruby in.

"I'm suddenly in the mood to take a trip up the hill," Brett said. He stood and grabbed his truck keys from the key holder on the wall. "Anyone else care to join me?"

"What's up the hill?" Lester asked.

"He's talking about the Dogwood House," Maggie said. "Where all of you are staying. Maybe we can smooth things over a little."

"I'm game. I'll follow you," Ruby said. She was the first one back out the door. Moments later, the convoy of parents pulled up in front of the stately

Dogwood House. Maggie slid out of the truck and waited for Lester, Anne, and Ruby to join her.

"We need to have a game plan before we go in there," Brett said.

"I think we speak as calmly and clearly as possible," Maggie suggested.

"What do we say?" Anne asked.

"I think we let someone do the talking for all of us," Lester suggested. He turned to Ruby. "Would you mind, Miss Cobb? It might help since you aren't technically related to any of us."

"Please, call me Ruby," she said. "And of course, I will be happy to do anything you need."

"I think yours might be the calmest voice," Lester said. "Perhaps you can convey to her the need to relax and let the kids get married without further incident."

"I think he's right," Brett said. "Ruby, you are the most detached from all this emotion we are all experiencing now. We need to make it clear to her what will happen if she causes any further damage to the wedding preparations."

"Do you want me to go as far as to threaten her with a possible arrest?" Ruby asked.

"Absolutely," Brett said bluntly. "Because that's where this goes next. She's wreaking havoc on these kids' plans. I don't want to make threats, and I don't intend to, but I will call the law on this woman if she keeps it up."

"I'm with you there," Lester said. "We may be the stepfathers, but we have just as much to lose if our children suffer anymore from this mess."

"Anne," Maggie said quietly. "What are your thoughts?"

Anne wiped her eyes again and turned to Ruby. "I want you to tell her that she has one more chance," she said clearly. "It doesn't matter how big or how small. One more foul up, and she will not be welcome at the wedding. And if we must use the police to enforce that, then so be it."

"Do we need to talk to Suzan and Bradley before we take this step?" Maggie asked suddenly. "It just popped into my head that they're not aware of what we're about to do."

"I don't think we should bother them with this right now," Anne said.

"I think my wife is right," Lester agreed.

"Then let's get this over with," Ruby said.

"Maybe we should fill Gretchen in on what's going on," Brett said. "We can tell her that Albert doesn't need to try to make us leave."

"Who is that?" Lester asked.

"He's Gretchen's handyman," Maggie explained as they walked toward the back door. "And you don't need to worry about it, sweetheart. I texted Gretchen before we left the house. She's expecting us."

The four of them followed Ruby toward the back door. They walked solemnly without speaking another word to each other. Ruby knocked softly on the screen door, then pulled it open. Albert opened the door for her and nodded his head. He didn't speak a word, but it was clear he knew what was going on.

Maggie went in behind Lester, surprised to see Bill was already seated at the bar in the kitchen. "You're too late," he said, shaking his head. "She's taken off."

"But your rental car is outside," Anne pointed out. "Where did she go?"

"Beats me," Bill said, raising his voice. "She went out earlier, came home and then left again. This time, as far as I know, she took off on foot. She's probably been picked up by some truck driver or something at this point."

"Mr. Logan," Brett said firmly. "Are you reporting your wife is a missing person?"

"I'm saying she's gone," Bill said. "And I don't know where she went."

"Mr. Logan went to retrieve his wife a few minutes ago," Gretchen said, appearing in the kitchen for the first time. "When he opened the door to their room, she was gone along with some of her things."

"And nobody saw her leave?" Lester asked.

Bill shook his head. "No one saw her go," he said. Maggie couldn't tell if he was answering with sarcasm or frustration. "All I know is she's not here."

"Then maybe we should go looking for her," Anne suggested. "It's after dark and Sandra isn't exactly thirty years old anymore."

"I will thank you not to insult my wife," Bill said.

Anne cringed and held tightly to her husband's hand. "I wasn't insulting your wife," she said. "We came here to have a discussion with her, but we meant no harm."

"Well, maybe she somehow she got wind of your intentions," Bill said. "And she decided to take off before you could get here."

"Surely you don't blame us for her leaving," Maggie said. "How would she know we were on our way over?"

"I don't know who to blame," Bill said, waving his hand in the air. He turned and stared intently at Maggie. "But you saw today what she's capable of. I suppose I don't blame all of you for coming here to give her the business."

"We had no intention of giving her the business," Ruby said. "But we did plan to firmly set some boundaries with her. She has already taken big steps to ruin this wedding. None of us want to see that happen."

"And who are you exactly?" Bill asked Ruby.

"She's the owner of the venue where the wedding will still take place," Brett said calmly. "No matter what waves and ripples your wife causes, at least we know the wedding will go on. Ruby is family."

"I suppose I should be grateful to you for that," Bill said. Maggie noticed an empty shot glass in front of him for the first time. The man had clearly been drinking and that likely wasn't going to help matters at all.

FIVE

"Hey, folks," Brett said after a few more minutes of chatting. "I don't mean to interrupt or anything, but I think all of us need to get in our cars and go looking for Mrs. Logan. If she's out there walking around, who knows what trouble she might find herself in."

"Maybe we should just let her walk it off," Lester suggested.

"I'm not trying to be pushy or anything," Brett said. "But these are the Ozarks. There are plenty of wild animals roaming around and the temperatures have already begun to dip. I don't think she has any business wandering around in the dark."

"Maybe you're right," Lester said. "I'm just so angry about all this mess I can't think straight. But I don't want anything bad to happen to her, no matter how angry I am at her."

"Fine," Bill said. "Let's get this over with."

"Why don't you ride with me, buddy?" Brett suggested.

"I can drive myself," Bill said. "After all, she is my wife."

"I'm afraid I'm going to have to agree with the former sheriff," Gretchen said, punctuating her words.

"You've had too much to drink to go out driving right now, Mr. Logan. Better to ride along with someone else for the time being."

Maggie followed Brett and the others outside. She climbed into Ruby's truck, giving Brett more room to place the slightly inebriated man into the passenger seat of his own pickup. After a quick discussion, they each agreed on an area to search. Even Albert climbed into a vehicle and headed out for a quick look.

"I can't believe she took off on foot," Ruby said when they headed down the road toward the lake. "She really is good at causing problems for other people, isn't she?"

"I'm surprised she took off on foot as well," Maggie said. "Although, I have to admit, I think it's a bit of a stunt on her part."

"A stunt? You think she did this to cause more trouble?" Ruby asked.

"I absolutely do think that she did this to cause more trouble," Maggie said. "She is the most entitled, petulant woman I have ever encountered. She is determined to ruin this wedding."

"But why?" Ruby asked, shaking her head. She drove slowly down the road, searching for any sign of Sandra. "Why would she do this?"

"Because she's not the center of attention," Maggie said. "I know I sound like an armchair psychologist right now, but that's the only explanation I can find. Lester and Anne seemed to get along with Bill just fine. Sandra is the only problem they have between them."

"The way she came into the donut shop this morning and insisted that Suzan was her daughter," Ruby said, shaking her head. "I suppose that shed some light on how she thinks. I can appreciate her taking on a parental role, but this is too much."

They continued to drive until they reached the lake, then slowly made their way through the maze of roads around it. When they emerged, nearly an hour had passed.

"I'm surprised we haven't heard anything from the others," Maggie said. "I wonder if someone found her?"

"I was thinking that same thing," Ruby said. "But I'm sure we would have heard something by now if they had."

"Where do we go now?" Maggie asked.

"Well, since we all agreed to meet back at the Dogwood House when we were finished searching, I guess we can just head back there," Ruby said. "Even with an hour gone, there's no way she could have made it out any further than this."

"Unless someone picked her up," Maggie said.

"Right," Ruby agreed. She turned her pickup toward the way they'd come and headed back toward the bed and breakfast. When they pulled into the driveway, they were surprised to see everyone was already back.

"Well?" Lester asked as soon as Maggie climbed out of Ruby's pickup. "Did you see anything?"

"No, we didn't," Maggie said, shaking her head. "I'm afraid we found no sign of her."

"This isn't good," Anne said. "This isn't good at all."

Maggie was surprised to see Bill resting his head against the side of Brett's truck. He said nothing about where his wife might have gone, or about the fact that no sign of her had been found.

"What do we do now?" Ruby asked.

"Now we call the sheriff and begin the process of filing a missing person's report," Brett said soberly. "Bill tried her cell phone several times while we were searching for her, but she didn't answer. I think we have to take this matter seriously."

"My wife is missing," Bill said at last. "She's gone missing, and I don't know where to find her."

"That's okay," Lester said, resting his hand on his shoulder. "We'll find her. Brett here is going to call in law enforcement. We'll make sure she's safe and sound."

"I don't know if that's going to do any good," Bill said, resting his head against the truck again.

"I think you need to go straight to bed." Maggie nodded to Ruby, then stepped close to Bill, hooking her arm under his. Ruby followed suit. Soon the women guided him across the driveway and up the porch to the back door.

"I'll make sure he gets to bed safely," Albert said, following them inside. Maggie stepped back and waited while he took control of this situation. By the time they walked out of the room together, it was clear Bill was close to passing out.

"Now what?" Lester said.

"Now we have a very difficult phone call to make," Ruby said. "We're going to have to call Bradley and Suzan and let them know Sandra is missing."

"They're going to postpone the wedding," Anne said. "Aren't they?"

"I think it's the only thing they can do," Maggie said softly. "But that doesn't mean it will be forever. Once the police get involved, I'm sure Sandra will be found quickly."

"I sure hope you're right," Lester said. "I don't want anything to happen to her, but I suppose she finally got her wish."

"Which was?" Ruby asked.

"She has been determined to ruin this wedding from the get-go," Lester said, shaking his head. "Tonight, she finally got her way."

SIX

"Tell me again about your relationship to the missing woman," Sheriff Cheryl Cornelius said to Maggie. They were seated in the kitchen of the Dogwood House. Maggie felt the frustration and fatigue of the day catching up with her.

"She is the stepmother of my son's fiancée," Maggie said. "As I have already explained to you."

"Look, Mrs. Mission," Sheriff Cornelius said. She leaned forward and rested her elbows on her legs. "I understand that your husband was once the sheriff of this county, but I'm new to the area. I don't know you and I didn't know him. You are going to have to talk to me like any other citizen."

"I'm not sure I like what you're insinuating there," Maggie said.

"I'm not insinuating a single thing," Sheriff Cornelius countered. "I have a missing woman and a family dynamic that I'm not very comfortable with. To top it off, I have you resisting my questions."

"I'm not resisting your questions," Maggie said. "I've already answered them three times."

"That feels like a bit of resistance to me," the sheriff said. She stood up and walked to the counter, then poured herself another glass of water from the pitcher Gretchen had set out before she went to bed. Maggie glanced up at the clock on the wall. It was five minutes past midnight.

"I had never met Sandra before this morning," Maggie explained. "I knew who she was, but we had not met formally. I suppose we still haven't formally met."

"So, what is it that you're considering happened this morning if it wasn't a meeting?" Sheriff Cornelius asked.

"She came into my donut shop," Maggie said. "She was shouting and accusing us of a number of things."

"I'm sure that made you angry."

"Of course it did," Maggie said. "Once I figured out what she was getting at, it made me very angry. I had already known from my future daughter-in-law that her stepmother could be a bit difficult, but this was a lot more than I expected."

"Where were you earlier this evening?" the sheriff said.

"Once again, I was with my husband until Anne and Lester showed up at our house. Ruby came along as well," Maggie said. "The five of us decided together to come here and have a talk with Sandra."

"Were you alone at any point?" Sheriff Cornelius asked.

"Absolutely not," Maggie said.

"What were you going to do when you confronted Sandra?"

"The five of us planned to tell her that she needed to back off," Maggie said. "We planned to tell her that her behavior so far has been atrocious, and that we wanted to get through the wedding without any more theatrics."

"She made you very angry, didn't she?" Sheriff Cornelius continued to press Maggie.

"Angry, embarrassed, confused," Maggie said. "All of the above. I've never seen a rational human being act that way."

"And then you found out that she visited the home of your son's wedding planner," the sheriff said. "And that prompted the wedding planner to quit on the spot."

"Yes, that's what happened."

"How did the rest of your group react to this news?"

"As I explained before, Anne and Lester were the ones who brought us the news," Maggie said. "Ruby showed up because that's the kind of relationship we have."

"So, she just showed up at your house?" the sheriff said.

"Yes, she just showed up at our house at the same time Anne and Lester were there," Maggie said.

"And that's not unusual to you?"

"Absolutely not," Maggie said. "Remember, Ruby had been there at the donut shop early this morning when Sandra made her first appearance. She didn't even bother to call before she showed up, knowing that wasn't necessary. She's my best friend who happened to stop by."

"The five of you together decided to pay her a visit," the sheriff said again.

"As I explained before," Maggie began.

"You know, you don't have to say that every time," Sheriff Cornelius said. "I understand that this isn't the first time you've told me this story."

"Then why are you asking the questions all over again?" Maggie said. She stifled a yawn by pressing the back of her hand against her mouth.

"Because this is part of my job," Sheriff Cornelius said. "I would think you would know that having been married to a former sheriff."

"I think you're wasting time," Maggie said. She sat up suddenly. "I was not alone at any point this evening. I have not done anything to Mrs. Logan. In fact, I wasn't informed that she was missing until we arrived here a few hours ago."

"How am I wasting time?"

"Because you're conducting this same interrogation over and over again," Maggie said. "The woman is out there on foot. Who knows what has happened to her at this point."

"What makes you think my deputies aren't out there looking for her at this very moment?"

"I have no doubt your deputies are out there already," Maggie said. "But I feel like you would serve this situation better by being out there yourself."

"Maybe I think you and the other parents had something to do with her disappearance," the sheriff said suddenly.

"You think the five of us kidnapped her and threw her out on the side of the road somewhere," Maggie said. She couldn't help herself. She sat back in her seat and began to laugh, covering her face with her hands. "No, of course we didn't have anything to do with her disappearance. None of us want that. We want this wedding to go off without a hitch for our children. We just want Mrs. Logan to calm down and stop behaving like a bull in a China shop."

"Now that you mention it, the five of you together could definitely have overpowered her."

"Sure, we could have," Maggie said. "But we didn't. Not one of us would ever do that."

"Still, you were willing to threaten her."

"Yes, with the police if she didn't behave herself," Maggie said. "Are you forgetting what she did to that poor woman's house in Hunter Springs? Not only did she force the wedding planner to quit, but she tore her house apart in the process."

"And that made you very upset," the sheriff said.

"Exactly where are you from?" Maggie asked. "Because you sure don't behave like any law enforcement officer I've ever met before."

"I think we're done here," the sheriff said suddenly. "You are dismissed."

"Does that mean I can go home?" Maggie asked.

"No," the sheriff said. "It means you can send in Ruby. I want to ask her more questions."

Maggie stood up and headed for the small living room off the kitchen. She knew the house like the back of her hand, despite the many changes Gretchen had made to it over the years. When she entered the room, four pairs of eyes glanced up at her.

"She wants to talk to you again, Ruby," Maggie announced.

"You've got to be kidding me," Brett said. His tone was rare, and Maggie could tell he was on the edge of his anger. "How incompetent is this woman?"

"Be careful," Lester said. "I have a feeling she's listening to everything we're saying."

"Let her listen," Brett said. "I've never experienced this with a law enforcement officer. She's accomplishing nothing by asking the five of us the same questions over and over again."

"I would like to go to bed," Anne said. Maggie glanced over at Suzan's mother and felt a sudden wave of sympathy. The woman rested her head against her husband's shoulder. She appeared as close to a wilted flower as any human being Maggie had ever seen.

SEVEN

Maggie finally retired to her bed around two o'clock in the morning. After a brief text exchange, it was determined that Naomi and Myra would open the donut shop the following morning so Maggie and Ruby could take the day off.

Brett, however, was determined to go in for at least part of the day. Maggie slept in and then forced herself to get out of bed and take a shower. Her phone rang as she was towel drying her hair. She was surprised to see Ruby calling her so early.

"How is it going?" Ruby asked.

"I just got up," Maggie said. "How about you?"

"I had to do some chores on the farm, but I slept in, too. I checked in with Naomi and things are going just fine at work."

"I'm sure we're going to hear about everything from Orson when we get back," Maggie said.

"Orson is working the counter."

"He is? I didn't expect that."

"Naomi said he insisted," Ruby said. "Even Myra couldn't get him to sit down."

"That's really nice of him," Maggie said, making the mental note to pick up a pound of Orson's favorite candy.

"Have you spoken with Bradley and Suzan?" Ruby asked.

"No, but they are due here in less than an hour," Maggie said. "Bradley agreed to take off after the morning rush. He said that the two of them have something they want to discuss with me."

"They're going to cancel the wedding," Ruby said. "Is that what you think is going on?"

"At least postponing it," Maggie said. "If they do cancel it, I'm going to suggest that they drive to Kansas and elope."

"Why Kansas?" Ruby asked.

"Because it's the opposite direction of where Bill and Sandra live," Maggie said.

"You still think she's pulling some sort of a stunt, don't you?"

"I do," Maggie said quickly. "I think this is all part of her master manipulation game."

"I don't know," Ruby said.

"What else are we supposed to think?" Maggie argued. "Nothing she has done so far has been about anything else. I think that's why Sheriff Cornelius spent so much time last night going over everything with us. None of it makes sense, even to her."

"Perhaps you're right," Ruby said. "At the very least, I think it started out as a stunt."

"Are you're worried someone picked her up?"

"That's exactly what I'm worried about."

"What are you doing for lunch?" Maggie asked, quickly changing the subject.

"I was just about to ask you the same thing," Ruby said. "I was going to invite you out, but if Bradley and Suzan are going to be there shortly, it might make more sense for me to come over."

"Brett will be home before lunch," Maggie said.

"That's even better," Ruby said. "I'd like for the three of us to sit down and talk about everything before we're around Lester, Anne, and Bill again."

"You just want to talk to Brett and me?"

"I trust the three of us more than I trust people I just met," Ruby said. "I'll bring lunch. I'll be there around twelve-thirty."

"That sounds good to me," Maggie ended the phone call.

She hustled to get ready. As she brushed out her hair, she thought about Ruby's words. She knew she could trust her husband and her best friend, but the truth was, she had only just met Suzan's family. And while she trusted Suzan completely, she didn't know enough about the others to cast judgment. Perhaps Ruby's idea was wise. Maybe the three of them needed to sit down and discuss things together.

Thirty minutes later, Suzan knocked on the back door. "Come on in," Maggie said. "You're going to have to learn you don't need to knock." She moved closer to the two of them and wrapped her son and future daughter-in-law in a big bear hug. "I'm so sorry things have gotten so complicated."

"It's not your fault," Bradley said. From the redness in his eyes, it was clear he hadn't gotten much sleep, either. Suzan's face was splotched with red, and her skin was puffy.

"Really," Suzan said. "Not a bit of this is your fault. If anything, it's mine."

"How can you think this is your fault?" Maggie asked, gesturing for them to take a seat at the kitchen table. "You have no control over what a grown woman does."

"We should have planned a smaller wedding," Suzan said, shaking her head. To Maggie's surprise, no tears filled her eyes. She stared at the wall past

Maggie's head. Clearly, the young woman was cried out and numb.

"She's been saying that all morning," Bradley said.

"Suzan, let me give you a little bit of advice," Maggie said. "In life, there are plenty of opportunities to take responsibility for things. but it serves no one if you take the blame for something that isn't your fault."

"I can't help but feel responsible for this," Suzan said.

"Of course you feel responsible, but that doesn't mean that you are. In a situation like this, the most helpful thing is to assign blame where it belongs. Your stepmother seems to be a pretty awful human being."

"Mom, she's missing," Bradley said.

Maggie held up her hands and nodded. "I'm aware. That's the reason I was up until two this morning trying to convince the new sheriff that I had nothing to do with it. But I'm still not convinced that this isn't a big stunt on Sandra's part."

"You think she took off on purpose?" Bradley asked.

"I'm not convinced she didn't," Maggie said. "Of course, if she is in danger, I want the full force of the law put into finding her and bringing her home safely."

"I'm of the same mindset," Suzan said. "I spoke to my dad this morning and he's scared to death that something bad happened to his wife. I wish I felt sympathy, but I don't."

Bradley nodded. "I agree that your stepmother is a difficult person, but I don't think any harm should come to her for it."

"Neither do I," Maggie said. "We have to tread carefully here. Right now, I am not convinced she's actually missing. Ruby, however, thinks she is."

"What, Aunt Ruby thinks she's been kidnapped or something?" Bradley asked.

"She thinks someone picked her up," Maggie said. "After the stunt of running off on foot."

"That's the most I would believe," Suzan said. "Honestly, this just feels like another chance for her to make our lives difficult."

"This isn't fair," Maggie said. "It's not fair the two of you are considering what I know you are considering."

"Oh, we're no longer considering," Bradley said. "We came over here to let you know in person that we will not be having a wedding after all."

"That's not the answer," Maggie said. She was shocked at her own calm demeanor. "You need to elope."

"You want us to run off and get married," Suzan said. She perked up for the first time. "Like, by ourselves?"

"Of course, I would give my right arm to be there," she said. "But with everything else that's going on, the two of you deserve to have the wedding you want, on your own terms."

"We can't do anything until this situation with Sandra is resolved," Bradley said.

"And that's very reasonable," Maggie said. "But I don't think Sandra is going to meet a terrible end. She will be back once she's sure she has punished all of us enough. And when she comes back, she's going to expect to take over the wedding herself. That's when the two of you need to take a stand."

"How long do you think she'll keep this up?" Suzan asked.

"I have no idea," Maggie said. "But I bet she doesn't last beyond two or three days. She is too determined to cause problems for other people. She won't be able to stand it long enough to be away much longer."

"I hope you're right, Mom," Bradley said. "I hope she's pulling a prank on everyone and not missing in the criminal sense."

"I don't know who she would have arranged it with," Suzan said. "But I bet she's sitting in some luxurious hotel room somewhere soaking her feet while the rest of us run around like chickens with our heads cut off."

"That's exactly what I think she wants," Maggie said. "I hope I'm right, because if she is missing, that isn't a happy ending, either."

"But even when she comes back," Bradley continued. "You think we should cancel the wedding?"

"I think you need to do something," Maggie said. "Because none of this is going to change. As long as there's a wedding, I'm afraid Sandra is going to do everything within her power to try to ruin it. Go get married and start your lives together. We can plan a big reception for the summer. Only then, you can decide who gets to come and who doesn't."

EIGHT

Bradley and Suzan left shortly after ten. Suzan had meetings to go to for her upcoming new job and Bradley was determined to help Zeke out at the donut shop in Hunter Springs. Maggie decided to spend a little bit of time on her laptop before Ruby and Brett arrived.

She began to search for venues in neighboring states that would make elopement easy on her children. She finally settled on Arkansas as the ideal state, then texted the information to her son. Afterward, she looked up a map of the area surrounding the Dogwood House. She traced the routes they had taken the night before in search of Sandra. "There's no way we would have missed her," she said, pushing herself back from her desk.

She wondered who might have been in on the act with the woman. Clearly, she had planned it out. Someone must have picked her up then dashed her away to a safe location where she would sit while everyone else worried about her safety. She closed her laptop lid and stared out the window for a moment before the ring of her cell phone in the kitchen interrupted her thoughts.

Maggie sprinted down the hall to the kitchen and picked up her phone. To her surprise, it was the Dogwood Mountain Sheriff's Department. "Mrs. Mission," Sheriff Cheryl Cornelius's voice boomed into the speaker.

"This is Maggie," she said. "What can I do for you, Sheriff?"

"I just wanted to inform you that an article belonging to Sandra Logan was found about twenty-five feet off of the highway close to the lake. Specifically, a shoe," the sheriff said. "I've already spoken with Bill and he identified it as one of the pair his wife was wearing that day."

"Oh, dear," Maggie said soberly. "That means someone did take her, doesn't it?"

"It appears so," the sheriff said. Maggie was surprised by the lack of sarcasm in the sheriff's voice.

"This has just become a very serious case, hasn't it?"

"Yes, it has," the sheriff said. "Look, Mrs. Mission, I understand all of you have solid alibis for last night, and I'm not saying that I suspect you are guilty of foul play. Somehow, given what I've learned about your husband from speaking with some of his former coworkers here, I tend to think the pair of you are above board citizens. But, if there's anything you know about her disappearance, now is the time to tell me."

"Until a moment ago, I didn't believe she had disappeared," Maggie said. "After that woman's behavior, I was convinced this was all part of some big, elaborate stunt."

"I've confirmed a lot of the details you shared with me about Sandra's antics," Sheriff Cornelius continued. "I can understand why you think that way, but, in my professional opinion, someone did take her against her will."

"Do you have any evidence aside from the missing shoe?"

"We've uncovered a set of vehicle tracks from where the shoe was located," the sheriff said. "We've determined that it came from a small, four-cylinder vehicle. The width of the tires indicated as such. We think someone spotted her walking, then got out and forced her into their vehicle."

"I feel just awful for doubting that she is in real danger," Maggie said, though she wasn't sure why she confessed it to the sheriff.

"It is definitely a strange case," Sheriff Cornelius said. "I will give you that."

"What happens now?" Maggie said. "How can we help locate her?"

"By telling me anything that comes up that you deem suspicious," the sheriff said. "Or if there are any details you remember about last night, let me know immediately. I'm sure you're aware that in kidnapping cases, the first forty-eight hours are essential."

"I am quite aware of that," Maggie said. She nodded her head solemnly. "I know that after the first couple of days, a person's chances of survival after an abduction go way down."

"And we've already lost more hours than we are aware of," Sheriff Cornelius said. "We have a four-hour window in which we think she was taken."

"And no witnesses," Maggie said.

"None whatsoever."

"Have you told my husband?"

"I just got off the phone with him," Sheriff Cornelius said. "I made it a point to call you personally."

"I understand you still have to investigate us," Maggie said. "You called to tell me just to hear my reaction."

"Something like that," Sheriff Cornelius said. "I'm doing my job, Mrs. Mission."

"Of course you are," Maggie said. "I don't blame you one bit. You have to do what you have to do. I just hope your efforts bring Sandra home safely."

"Even after everything she's done?" the sheriff asked.

"Even after everything she's done," Maggie said. "She's still a human being. She might not be my favorite person on the planet, but I don't wish her any harm." She was quite aware that the sheriff had just set another trap for her, and she didn't care.

"Fair enough," the sheriff said. "I will leave you to the rest of your day. By the way, why aren't you at work?"

"Because someone prevented me from going to bed until after two in the morning," Maggie said. "My workday begins at five."

"Got it," Sheriff Cornelius said. "Just know I will be in touch soon." Maggie ended the phone call just as she heard Brett's pickup pull into the driveway. She opened the back door for him and waited for him to get out of his truck.

"Did she call you?" Brett said before he walked into the house.

"Yes, we just ended our phone call," Maggie said. "They found a shoe."

"That's not a good sign," Brett said. His face was drawn and sober.

"I know," Maggie said. "I'm afraid something bad has happened to her."

"That just makes all of this so terrible," Brett said, shaking his head. "I can only imagine how Suzan is taking all of this."

"I think Suzan is in a state of shock already," Maggie said. "She and Bradley left just over an hour ago. I could tell by her face that she had been crying, but I don't think she had any tears left."

"I wonder if they know about the shoe," Brett said.

"I'm not sure," Maggie said. "I heard about it after they left."

"I don't like any of this."

"Neither do I," Maggie said. "As much as I detest that woman, I don't want anything to happen to her. And I hate the shadow this will cast over the kids' wedding."

"That's not what I mean," Brett said. "With the way the sheriff spoke to me, I'm quite sure we're on the list of suspects."

"You think we're suspects?" Maggie asked, astonished.

"Of course we are," Brett said. "She isn't trying to look for anyone else."

"Wait a minute," Maggie said, half closing her eyes. "You're saying Sheriff Cornelius suspects that you and I had something to do with Sandra Logan's disappearance?"

"Not only us," Brett said. "She suspects Lester and Anne as well."

"Did she tell you this?" Maggie asked.

"Not in so many words," Brett said. "But I know the jargon. She asked me to make sure I share anything else I think of with her."

"That's the same thing she said to me as well."

"My point exactly."

"No, no," Maggie said, shaking her head. "That doesn't mean anything. She wants us to simply call her if we remember any other details about last night."

"It's like a catch phrase, Maggie," Brett said. "It's the same thing I used to say to suspects, hoping to make them feel comfortable enough to knock them off their game."

"That's not true," Maggie said. "Is it? Did you really used to say that to people?"

"Of course I did," Brett said. "Criminals get lazy when they're comfortable. She wants us to be comfortable."

"Because she thinks we are going to mess up and she'll get us?"

"You don't believe me, do you?" Brett said.

"It's not that I don't believe you, honey," Maggie said. "It's just that I think you're wrong about what she meant."

"I'll tell you what," Brett said, pulling his cell phone out of his back pocket. "Call Lester and ask him what the sheriff said to them. I would almost guarantee you she said practically the same thing."

"I don't have Lester's number," Maggie said.

"Allow me," Brett said, tapping on his screen with a flourish. A second later, Maggie heard the dial tone. Brett put his phone on speaker.

"Hello," Lester answered a moment later. "Is that you, Brett?"

"Sure is," Brett said. "I just wondered if you or Anne got a call from Sheriff Cornelius this afternoon?"

"Both of us did," Lester said. "How about you guys?"

"Same here," Brett said. "Say, what did she have to tell you?"

"She just wanted to let us know that Sandra's shoe had been found," Lester said.

"That's the same thing she said to us," Brett said. His eyes remained locked on Maggie's as he spoke. "Anything else?"

"No, just that if we think of anything else, we are to call her immediately and let her know," Lester said. "I got the feeling she wanted to make sure we were in the know."

"That's about the same thing she said to me, buddy," Brett said. "I definitely think she suspects foul play now."

"I'm glad for that. As long as she doesn't suspect any of us, of course," Lester said with a chuckle.

NINE

Ruby arrived a short time later, carrying in three baskets of food. Maggie found herself temporarily distracted from the stress at hand.

"You brought all this for just three people?" Brett asked, peeking into one of the baskets.

"I told Bradley about the food," Ruby said. "I figured they might swing by a little later and pick up leftovers."

"That was very thoughtful of you," Maggie said.

"I hope you're in the mood for something rustic and comforting," Ruby continued. She pulled large, still-warm biscuits from under a towel and set them on the counter. Next, she uncovered a pot of chicken and dumplings soup. "I whipped up a batch of our latest apple streusel donuts for dessert."

"That sounds perfect," Brett said. He reached for a biscuit and swiped it before Ruby could smack his hand.

"Hey," Ruby said. "Wait for us to sit at the table at least."

"Now Ruby," Brett said as he plucked off a piece of the biscuit and popped it in his mouth. "You've known me far too long to expect me to wait."

"Did you get a phone call from the sheriff?" Maggie asked when she couldn't stand to wait any longer.

"I did," Ruby said. "I assume both of you did as well."

"We all did." Brett nodded.

"I don't want to alarm you," Ruby said, glancing at Maggie. "But I think we're all on her short list of suspects."

"That's what Brett thinks, too," Maggie said.

"Then, if the former sheriff thinks so," Ruby said, rolling her head back. "I suppose it's true."

"Do you really think we are suspects?" Maggie said.

"I think it stands to reason that we are," Ruby said. "But I'm not worried about it. I know none of us did anything."

"What I don't understand is how can the sheriff think we're suspects when the timeline doesn't work," Maggie said.

"Because timelines shift," Brett said. "Give it another week with more testing done, and it's possible that the window of abduction changes."

"That's what I was thinking," Ruby said.

"Someone took her, though," Maggie said. "We already know who didn't do it. What we have to figure out is, who did."

"I bet it was a random stranger," Ruby said. "Maybe they happened upon an older woman walking around in an agitated state and they seized the opportunity."

"I don't think it was someone random," Brett said. "We all know those roads like the backs of our hands. No one just happens upon someone walking."

"What are you saying then?" Ruby asked.

"Something doesn't feel right," Brett said. He was quiet for a moment, then nodded his head. "Something isn't adding up. I think whoever took Sandra knew her."

"Do you suspect her husband?" Maggie asked.

"I'm not sure yet," Brett said. "I do think I would like more of a chance to talk to him."

"There are only so many people who knew she was gone in the first place," Maggie reminded them. "There were the three of us of course, then Anne and Lester. But you also have Bill. We both know Gretchen and Albert don't have anything to do with this."

"It sounds as if you're already considering Bill a suspect," Ruby said to Maggie.

"I don't know what I think at the moment," Maggie said. "I'm still wrapping my head around the idea that the sheriff suspects any of us."

"Right," Ruby agreed. "It is difficult to understand why, given the fact that we are all our own alibis."

"Do you think she suspects we all worked together?" Maggie asked.

"I think she suspects us parents," Brett said.

"But she said the same thing to Ruby that she said to the rest of us," Maggie pointed out.

"You don't think I'm a suspect?" Ruby asked.

"Not the same way we are," Brett said. "What I mean by that is, I'm afraid Sheriff Cornelius suspects that Maggie and I along with Lester and Anne probably plotted to kidnap Sandra. Your part would be merely as a lookout or something along those lines. I doubt she even thinks you know what is going on."

"Okay, hang on," Maggie said. "If Sheriff Cornelius suspects we took Sandra somewhere, why isn't she beating down the door demanding to know where she is? If I suspected someone kidnapped another human being, I wouldn't let up until I found out where that person was being held."

"Maybe she doesn't really think it was any of us, but she has nowhere else to look right now," Ruby mused.

"That sounds about right," Brett said.

Maggie was quiet for a moment. She ladled some soup into her bowl and dumped her biscuit into the broth. "I have no proof that Bill was involved, but I do think that's a pretty good place to start looking."

"How do you plan to do that?" Ruby asked.

"I suppose I'll have to have a talk with him," Maggie said. "But there is someone I intend to speak with first."

Following lunch, Maggie helped Ruby load the refrigerator with the food Bradley and Suzan would swing by to pick up later on. Brett had eaten so much he was napping on the couch, giving Maggie some time on her own.

"What are you doing now?" Ruby asked as Maggie searched the kitchen for her keys and cell phone.

"I plan to drive to Hunter Springs," Maggie announced.

"And do what exactly?" Ruby asked.

"I want to have a conversation with Alexandra," Maggie said. "Please don't try to stop me."

"I'm not going to try to stop you," Ruby said. "I'm going with you."

"That isn't necessary," Maggie said.

"Maybe not," Ruby said. "But it's safer. Why do you want to talk to her anyway?"

"Call it a hunch," Maggie said. "I want to hear from her exactly what happened with Sandra."

"What makes you think Alexandra will speak to you?" Ruby asked. "She has already made it clear there will be no return on the deposits."

"Right, I'm aware," Maggie said. "But I have some questions about the caterer. So far, I haven't heard anything about a cancelation with the catering firm. So, I have an excuse to visit."

"Don't you think that Bradley and Suzan are the ones handling all of this?" Ruby asked.

"I forgot to ask when they were here," Maggie said. "But I don't want to disturb them. I'll shoot a quick text to Bradley once I've spoken with Alexandra. Until then, you might say it's my excuse for visiting her."

"She might not trust that you want to have a simple talk with her," Ruby said. She followed Maggie out of the house and to her car. "She might even be a little suspicious given what Sandra just put her through."

"I've considered that possibility," Maggie said.

"You could just call her," Ruby suggested.

"I've already tried," Maggie said. She opened her car door and slid behind the wheel. "She wouldn't answer my call, not that I blame her."

"How do you plan to get in the front door?" Ruby asked.

"For one thing, there was another one hundred and fifty dollars due for the wedding," Maggie said. "I plan to give it to her."

"But she's not working the wedding anymore," Ruby pointed out as she stretched the seat belt over her lap.

"That doesn't mean she doesn't deserve it," Maggie said. "Our contract says that she deserves another one hundred fifty dollars for her efforts. I figured, if anything, it might go to help replace what Sandra broke in her house."

"You have a strange way of getting people to trust you," Ruby said.

TEN

Maggie pulled her car in front of a small white clapboard house just blocks from the Hunter Springs donut shop. She turned the engine off and pulled out her keys, then gazed at the house with a sigh.

"Are you sure you want to do this?" Ruby asked before they got out.

"I feel like I need to," Maggie said. "Besides, she does have some information we need. I don't have contact information for everyone."

"Whose are you missing?" Ruby asked.

"The wedding cake baker,"

"Don't you think you could get that from the caterer?"

"Maybe I could," Maggie said. "But that wouldn't serve all my purposes, would it?"

"I suppose not." Ruby chuckled.

Maggie stepped up onto the small brick walkway that led to the front door. Before she knocked, she looked around behind her, taking in the surroundings. Unlike many of the houses up and down the block, Alexandra's front porch was visible from almost a block away. She turned back to the door and knocked softly.

"Coming," a woman's voice called out. A second later, Alexandra cracked the front door. "What do you want?"

"Alexandra," Maggie said quickly. "I'm not here to cause trouble, but we still owe you a little bit for your services."

"You still owe me?" Alexandra asked, widening the crack a bit. Maggie could see her face.

"Yes, according to the contract, we still owe you money," Maggie said. "I'm here to pay you that amount."

"But why?" Alexandra said. "I wasn't going to push it. I just wanted to be done with this wedding."

"That is absolutely understandable," Ruby said behind Maggie.

"I don't think we've met," Alexandra said.

"We did, but it was months ago," Ruby said. "I'm Ruby, and I own the barn where the wedding is to be held."

"That's right," Alexandra said. "I'm so sorry. This week just has been so awful."

"May we come in?" Maggie asked. "I promise we won't stay long. I just want to see if I can get a couple of phone numbers from you while we're here."

"What phone numbers?" Alexandra asked curiously.

"For one, the caterer," Maggie said quickly. "And the baker. I couldn't find either number."

"Who is handling the wedding?" Alexandra asked, almost apologetically. She moved out of the way and opened the door.

"Basically, we are," Maggie said. "But there's been another complication."

"Let me guess," Alexander said. "The brides step-mother got to someone else."

"I'm not sure there's anyone she hasn't gotten to," Ruby said.

"But that's the thing," Maggie said. "I'm surprised the sheriff hasn't been in touch with you."

"The sheriff? What would the sheriff want with me?" Alexandra asked.

Maggie sucked in a breath. "As of last night, Sandra Logan has gone missing."

"Wait a minute," Alexandra said. "Sandra is missing?"

"Yes, she went for a walk last night," Maggie said. "And she wound up missing. They found a shoe belonging to her, but so far there's been no other trace."

"You don't suspect me, do you?" Alexandra asked.

"Of course not," Ruby said.

"Still, I would not be surprised if the police showed up here to ask you some questions," Maggie said. "We were up until two o'clock in the morning doing the very same thing."

"What about the wedding?" Alexandra asked.

"That's the main reason why I wanted to stop by today," Maggie said. She glanced at Ruby, hoping her friend wouldn't contradict anything she said. "I don't know if the wedding is going to go on as planned. If possible, I would like to postpone everything, based on what my son and Suzan decide they want to do."

"Wait here a minute," Alexandra said, disappearing down the hall. She returned with a thick envelope and handed it to Maggie. "Here's everything I have for your son's wedding."

"Thank you," Maggie said. "I take it the information for the caterers are in here?"

"Absolutely everything is in there," Alexander said. "And you can keep the balance. I truly don't need it."

"We were thinking that it might help to replace what Sandra broke when she was here," Ruby said.

"Oh, that won't be necessary," Alexandra said. "Her husband already came around and paid me an extra five hundred dollars."

"Bill came here?" Maggie asked.

"Yes, after he saw what his wife did," Alexandra confirmed.

"Bill witnessed what Sandra did here in your house?" Ruby asked casually.

"Yes, he was just up the road and came by to pick her up just in time," Alexandra said. "To be honest with you, I wonder how much worse things might have gotten if he hadn't been here so fast."

"Did he say if he had been sitting outside watching her or something?" Maggie asked.

"No, he told me that he anticipated she was going to cause some trouble," Alexandra said. "I think he figured out where she was headed and drove as fast as he could to try to prevent any more problems."

"I guess it's a good thing he got here when he did," Ruby said.

"When did he stop by?" Maggie asked. "To pay for the damage, I mean?"

"Oh, sometime before dinner yesterday," Alexandra said. "I had taken the day off, so I can't tell you exactly what time it was."

"Was he by himself?" Ruby asked.

"Yes, and he kept saying we don't want anything more to disturb this wedding. I assumed he meant all of you," Alexandra said.

"Honestly, I wasn't aware he'd stopped by, but he's not wrong. No one wants more drama," Maggie said. "Anyway, thank you. I'm so sorry for the trouble this caused you."

"Good luck with everything," Alexandra said, walking them to her front door.

Maggie drove in silence back to Dogwood Mountain. Still about five miles outside of town, Ruby turned into her seat with her arms folded. "What gives?"

"Pardon me?"

"You know what I mean," Ruby said. "You're never this quiet unless there's something on your mind. What's up with you?"

"I can't put my finger on it." Maggie shook her head. "But it's just like Brett was saying. There's something here that doesn't add up."

"None of this adds up," Ruby said. "For starters, why would anyone behave the way Sandra did? Unless maybe there's something wrong with her other than a bad attitude."

"You know, that's something I asked Bradley from the start," Maggie said. "Especially after the way she behaved at the donut shop. He said Sandra is smart as a whip and very capable."

"So then, she's really just a jerk?"

"It seems so," Maggie said. "I guess she's just a person who doesn't care about anyone besides herself, not even her own stepdaughter."

"Maybe it's because this is her stepdaughter," Ruby said. "Maybe there's some jealousy issues going on."

"I don't think so," Maggie said. "I just think she's a difficult person."

"It's amazing that Bill and Sandra are still married, then."

Maggie fell silent again. She gripped the steering wheel while thoughts raced through her mind. She was grateful to see the turnoff into Dogwood Mountain, driving the rest of the way home on autopilot.

"That's it," she said when she turned to pull into the driveway behind her house. "I think you just figured out what's really going on," Maggie said. "And why it's been so hard for any of us to make sense of it."

Ruby stared at her for a moment. "I haven't said anything useful in the last ten minutes. What exactly did I figure out?"

ELEVEN

Maggie rushed out of the car and headed straight for the back door. Still confused, Ruby followed her inside where Brett was seated at the kitchen table. "We need to go to the Dogwood House," Maggie said. "We need to go there right now."

"Sheriff Cornelius is on her way back to town," Brett announced.

"Is she's stopping by here?" Ruby asked from behind Maggie.

Brett nodded. "She said she'll be here in a couple of hours."

"All the more reason for us to go now," Maggie said. She walked past Ruby and stood by the still-open back door. "Come on. I'm not kidding."

"Why are we going back there?" Brett asked.

"I'll explain on the way," Maggie said. "But we've got to get there now before this thing gets even more out of hand."

"Maggie, slow down. What thing are you talking about?" Brett said, growing more frustrated with every word.

"Honey, trust me," Maggie said. "Aren't those the same words you used with me many times while you were still sheriff? Well, I'm asking for a little trust this time. Just follow me and let's go."

"I'll drive separately," Ruby announced, heading to her own pickup. Brett threw his hands in the air and followed Maggie outside, locking the door behind him. She went straight for her car. Brett reluctantly climbed into the passenger seat and secured his seat belt.

"Care to tell me what's going on now?"

"Ruby and I just left Hunter Springs. We had a little talk with the wedding planner."

"So, you fed me a ton of food then waited until I fell asleep before you decided to go interview the wedding planner?" Brett said.

"Of course," Maggie said. "It's better to ask for forgiveness than permission." She smiled at him, but he didn't respond in-kind.

"We're almost there," Brett pointed out.

"Just trust me," Maggie said again. "I don't have time to explain everything, but I don't think Sandra was kidnapped."

"Is that right?"

"Yes. I don't think she's in any danger at all. We just need to get to the bottom of this before Sheriff Cornelius comes along and ruins two good people's lives."

"Maggie," Brett said. "Don't get in over your head with this."

"That's exactly what I'm trying to prevent," Maggie said. She parked her car on the small grass area next to the driveway and waited for Ruby to pull in. "Follow my lead when we get inside."

Ruby nodded and exchanged quizzical looks with Brett. They approached the back door to the Dogwood House, and Gretchen opened the door before Maggie had a chance to knock. "I didn't expect the three of you," she said with a smile.

"Are Anne and Lester here?" Maggie asked.

"Yes, they're in the sitting room with Bill at the moment," Gretchen said. She opened the door and let the everyone inside. "Suzan and Bradley were just here. Tensions are running pretty high; I must warn you."

"I'm not surprised," Maggie said softly. "Everything is running out of control."

"Hopefully you can help put an end to that," Gretchen said. She led the way down the hall to the small sitting room close to the front living area.

"We didn't expect to see you so soon," Lester said brightly when Brett, Maggie, and Ruby walked into the small sitting room. "What brings you by?"

"We just wanted to check on how things are going," Maggie said. She could feel the pressure of Brett's glare on her. He stared hard, wondering what she was up to, but she ignored him and pressed

TO HAVE AND TO HOLED

forward anyway. "Did the kids make any concrete plans?"

"No. But they're discussing eloping," Anne said. She was clearly in a different mood than the men. "They said you suggested it."

"I did suggest it," Maggie said. "Although I know it's not what any of us want, it may be the only way for them to get through this without more problems."

"I don't see why they can't just go ahead with their wedding as planned," Bill said. "Just go through with it and then we'll leave this other matter with Sandra up to the police to figure out." Maggie turned slightly and looked over her shoulder at her husband. His gaze turned from a glare to confusion, then understanding in the span of a moment.

"You think they should go on with the wedding with your wife missing?" Brett asked.

"Well, I hate to be crass about it, but that's one major obstacle out of the way," Bill said with a shrug. "And we have no evidence that anything bad actually happened to Sandra."

"I can't believe you could suggest something so awful," Anne said. "Both of these men think the kids should press forward with the wedding. I can't get over that. One does not hold a wedding when one of the parents is missing."

"Says who?" Lester glanced at Bill and shrugged. "Like the man said, one major obstacle is out of the way for now."

"You better not let the sheriff here you two talk like that," Brett said. "She might think both of you had something to do with Sandra's disappearance."

"That wouldn't be good for anyone," Maggie said.

"If she winds up safe and sound, what difference does it make?" Lester asked.

"Gentlemen, I'm not sure if you understand the gravity of the situation," Brett said. "Kidnapping is a major offense. And if Sandra has suffered any injury of any kind, the charges will be even more serious."

"But if she isn't really missing," Bill said. "Surely they would let one off with a slap on the wrist."

"I highly doubt that," Maggie said. "Like my husband said, kidnapping is a serious charge."

"But what if Sandra herself declines to press charges?" Lester asked.

"It won't matter," Brett said. "Once the crime has been committed, the charges are out of the hands of the victim."

"Are you sure about that?" Bill asked.

"I'm quite sure," Brett said. "If you'll remember, I have a bit of experience in this sort of thing."

"Even if she's okay?" Bill repeated.

"Even if it was all a misunderstanding." Maggie cleared her throat. "Even if the whole purpose was to keep her somewhere safe until the wedding could proceed without her causing any more issues."

"What's that supposed to mean?" Anne asked, barely able to get the words out.

"I think you should ask your husband and former husband that question," Maggie said.

"I think I understand now," Ruby said. "Now would be the time to speak up, gentlemen. Sheriff Cornelius is on her way into town to talk to all of us."

"She is?" Lester asked. "Is she coming here?"

"Eventually, yes," Brett said. "She's on her way over to our house right now."

"Then why are you here?" Anne said.

"Because," Maggie said. "We just got back from Hunter Springs. Ruby and I paid Alexandra a visit."

"Oh, has she agreed to help out with the wedding again?" Anne said, finally perking up, despite the look she was giving her husband.

"No, she wants nothing to do with the wedding," Maggie said. "She did provide me with all of the paperwork and contact information, but that's not why we stopped by to see her."

"Care to share with the rest of the class?" Bill rolled his eyes.

"Because, I had some questions for her," Maggie said. "And I got some answers, answers that told me everything I needed to know about you, Bill."

"Is that how you figured it out?" Lester asked. He hung his head.

"Figured what out?" Anne shouted.

"Do you want to tell them, or should I?" Brett asked, resuming his authoritarian voice that reminded Maggie of the days he spent in uniform.

"She's not too far away." Bill sighed. "She's safe and sound."

"You know where Sandra is?" Anne asked, springing to her feet.

"They're the ones who took her," Maggie said.

"Lester, is that true?" Anne demanded. "Bill, did you do something to your wife?"

"We didn't do anything to her," Bill said, wringing his hands. "We just took her somewhere for a little, uh, wellness vacation."

"She's at a campground outside of Branson," Lester said at last.

"So, you did have something to do with it?" Anne gasped.

"Now, honey, don't get all upset at me," Lester said. "Bill asked me for some help, and I was very happy to oblige. Sandra was going to ruin that wedding one way or another."

"But you kidnapped her," Anne said. "You're going to go to prison for the rest of your lives."

"Maybe not." Brett glanced sideways at Maggie. "Maybe we can smooth everything out before the sheriff catches wind of this."

"And then what?" Ruby asked. "Convince her that it was all a big misunderstanding?"

"More or less, yes," Brett said.

"What happened?" Anne demanded to know. "No one is doing anything until I find out what really happened to Sandra."

"She went for a walk because I suggested she go away and miss the wedding if she was going to continue acting the way she had been," Bill explained.

"I helped him by stealing the keys from Albert," Lester said. "He took the little truck and caught up with Sandra after she took off on foot."

"But why was her shoe left on the side of the road?" Anne asked.

"Because, by the time I caught up with her, her heels were killing her feet," Bill said. "She was walking barefoot. I had to convince her to get into the truck with me, and she threw a shoe at me. I ducked and it didn't hit me, but I never picked it up."

"Why didn't you just tell the sheriff?" Ruby asked.

"Because we thought we could still get away with it," Bill admitted.

"Get away with what exactly?" Anne demanded.

"Sandra got mad when I asked her to take a small vacation at a cabin I booked for her way up in the mountains outside of Branson," Bill said. "It's a luxurious retreat and all she had to do was go there for a week and get waited on hand and foot, but she didn't want to."

"So, you put her in the truck and took her anyway?" Brett asked.

"And you covered for him," Maggie said to Lester.

"More or less," Lester agreed.

"Why didn't she just call and have someone come and get her?" Anne asked.

"Because maybe she didn't have her cell phone with her," Bill said. "And maybe cell phone service up there is pretty spotty at best so asking for help might be difficult."

"Then you marooned her at a resort in the hills until you decided it was time to come and get her?" Ruby asked.

"Just think of it as a grown-up timeout." Bill smiled.

"You're going to have to go get her," Anne said. "Both of you are going to have to apologize all over your- selves and pray that she doesn't decide to ruin your lives for what you've done."

"We'll head over there," Lester said. "We'll be gone more than a couple of hours, though."

"Then we'll stay here and explain everything to the sheriff," Brett said. "We'll do our best to smooth things over, but you better get on the road."

"She's going to kill us, you know," Lester said. "As soon as we show up there, she's going to have our heads."

"I don't want to hear a word about it," Anne said. "That's exactly what both of you have coming. I hope she tears into both of you worse than she's ever done before."

TWELVE

"I can't believe this day is finally here," Naomi whispered to Maggie in the kitchen at Ruby's farmhouse.

Maggie, dressed in her slip and robe, stirred creamer into her coffee. "I never thought we'd actually make it," she said. She paused, holding the spoon over the cup. "But then again, I should have never doubted it."

"I think it's a bit miraculous that Sandra chose not to press charges," Naomi said.

"You don't have to whisper," Suzan said, walking into the kitchen behind them.

"I wasn't whispering because I worried about you overhearing what I was saying," Naomi said. "I just didn't know who else was awake."

"I'm awake," Ruby announced.

"So am I," Myra said. She giggled as she poured a cup of coffee for herself. "Today is your wedding day." She sang the words and bumped Suzan lightly with her shoulder.

"I know," Suzan said, smiling wider than Maggie had ever seen her smile before. "It's incredible."

"When is your mother supposed to be here?" Ruby asked.

"By eight," Suzan said. "I'm still shocked she decided to go back to the bed and breakfast with Lester."

"You're not the only one," Maggie said.

"I just have to ask," Myra said. "Is everything going to be okay with everyone today?"

"Sandra has promised to be on her best behavior," Suzan said.

"I don't think that's what she means," Naomi said.

"It isn't," Myra said. "I meant with all your parents and Bradley's parents." She glanced sideways at Maggie.

"I think she's asking whether or not your father and stepfather are okay to be in the same room with me," Maggie said.

"Why, because you busted them for kidnapping?" Suzan chuckled. "Everything is fine. Trust me. After Sandra convinced Sheriff Cornelius not to throw the pair of them in jail, I think they decided to approach the rest of their lives with gratitude."

"That's one heck of a way to put it," Ruby said.

"I really didn't mean to cause any more trouble," Maggie said.

"Years from now, we're going to laugh about this whole fiasco," Suzan said. She drew in a breath and frowned. "But Maggie, think about it. If you hadn't figured out what was going on, and heaven forbid something really bad happened to Sandra, my father and stepfather would be facing years in prison."

"I still don't understand what tipped you off," Naomi said.

"At first, I didn't know either and I was there." Ruby laughed.

"It was the other day when we visited the wedding planner," Maggie said. "Alexandra told us that she thought it was strange Bill was close by after Sandra threw her fit."

"What, like he was waiting for her there or something?" Suzan asked.

"Kind of." Maggie nodded. "It didn't sit right with me when I learned that Bill was just a few minutes behind Sandra. It was almost as if he expected trouble out of her."

"He probably did," Naomi said. "Didn't he pretty much spend most of his time here cleaning up her messes?"

"Yes, and after all this time, it's probably not too hard for him to anticipate her next move." Suzan frowned.

Maggie chuckled. "I just got to thinking about times when Bradley was little, and I knew he was going to act up somewhere. After a couple of experiences, you learn how to predict your child's behavior."

"And you think Bill was predicting his wife's behavior?" Myra asked. "Is that it?"

"Essentially, yes," Maggie said. "That's why I think it was easy to figure out he was the one who picked her up and took her somewhere."

"My only question is, what did he think was going to happen when the wedding had come and gone, and he went to pick her up?" Naomi said.

"I think he decided he was just going to deal with that when it happened," Ruby said.

"Basically, don't ask for permission, just ask for forgiveness," Maggie said, completely familiar with the saying. She turned back to her coffee and took a long sip. "I'm just really glad your parents aren't angry with me."

"I'm really glad that long time out did my step-mother some good." Suzan laughed. "I mean, I've never seen her more sincere than she was last night when she gave me an apology."

"Sandra apologized to you?" Myra asked.

"With Dad standing in the doorway behind her, yes," Suzan said. "It reminded me of when I used to get in trouble and then had to go apologize to whomever I wronged."

"Maybe that timeout did teach her a lesson." Ruby smiled.

"Imagine needing a timeout at her age," Naomi said.

"So, when do we start getting ready?" Myra asked, changing the subject.

"As soon as we have breakfast," Ruby said. "Which, I promised I would serve when Anne arrived."

"While the women are having breakfast, what are the men up to?" Suzan asked.

"Well, Brett promised to take Bradley for a fancy shave and haircut this morning," Maggie said.

"Are Dad and Lester tagging along?" Suzan asked.

"Not this time," Ruby said. "I think your mom decided that was their punishment for kidnapping your stepmother. They have to miss out on the fun this morning and babysit Sandra, just to make sure she doesn't get in more trouble."

"That seems a little odd," Myra said. "Asking the two men that kidnapped her in the first place to watch her."

"They're also watching the kids," Maggie said.

"Oh, great. Are they watching the kids?" Myra asked. "Or are the kids watching them?"

THIRTEEN

By noon, the sun had risen high overhead. The sky was a deep blue cloudless marvel. Maggie noted that the photographer lifted his lens above his head and snapped several photos between family shots. For October, it was the perfect crisp fall day. Many of the outdoor photo sessions were taken against a backdrop of multicolored leaves on the still full trees in Ruby's woods.

Brett arrived shortly after breakfast with Bradley in tow. She was surprised to see Wyatt dressed to the nines and strapped in his car seat in the back seat of Brett's pickup. Wyatt smiled and gave her a thumbs up as he followed his father into the back of the barn where the wedding was set to take place.

"Okay, someone needs to get out a box of tissues for these two," Myra said, pointing to Maggie and Suzan.

Maggie glanced at Suzan and noticed a single tear streaking down her face. She blinked the tears back into her own eyes. "It's an emotional day," she said with a shrug. "I think both of us are feeling it."

"You're not the only one," Anne said. She stepped next to her daughter and swiped her finger under her eye. "Better get another tube of mascara while you're at it. Mine is already running."

"That's not good, Mom," Suzan said. "We're about to go to the barn."

"I know, but did you see little Wyatt dressed in his little suit?" Anne sniffed loudly to prevent another round of tears.

"You know, Wyatt gets something today he's never had before," Maggie said.

"What's that?" Myra asked.

"Another grandma," Maggie said, squeezing Anne lightly around her shoulders. "He's always only had me."

"Wyatt gets a lot of precious things today," Ruby said.

"Hey, who is that walking this way?" Anne asked. They stood in their dresses outside of Ruby's farmhouse watching the guests arrive.

"Well, given the way he's walking, I would say that's Orson," Myra said.

"Oh, boy," Naomi muttered.

"Why do you say that" Anne asked.

"Because he's got a look on his face," Naomi said. "I can see it from here."

"I wonder what he wants," Myra said.

"We're about to find out," Ruby said as Orson approached.

"Are you gals ready yet?" Orson said. He stopped and folded his arms over his chest. "You know everyone's waiting on you down there."

"We're not scheduled to be there for another ten minutes," Suzan said.

"That's when you had a wedding planner," Orson said. "Today, I'm your wedding planner. And I say it's time to hightail your fancy fannies down there. Let's go." He turned on his heel and marched back in the direction he came.

Maggie glanced at Suzan and shrugged. "I suppose we should follow him."

"I'm afraid what he'll do if we don't," Suzan whispered.

The parade of women followed Orson down to the barn. They slipped into the side entrance and headed straight for the ladies' powder room. Maggie and Anne teamed up and checked the bride head to toe. She seemed no worse for the wear given the short walk across the pasture.

"I can hear the music," Myra whispered.

"But I haven't seen dad or Lester yet," Suzan said, her eyes swimming with worry.

"Lester said they'd be here," Anne reassured her. "I heard Chloe when we walked in. I'm sure they're here."

"Come on, gals," Orson called outside of the bathroom door. "Don't make me come in there and get you."

"I can promise you he actually would," Myra said, not even bothering to whisper.

"I heard that, young lady," Orson said. "It's time."

Suzan glanced at Maggie then turned to her mother. They embraced quickly. Myra and Naomi headed out of the door first. Maggie and Anne followed. Anne hesitated, then poked her head back into the bathroom. "I just saw your dads," she whispered. "They're both here."

Maggie found her place next to Orson. He held out his arm and she circled her own carefully through it. Myra and Brett walked down the aisle first, followed by Zeke and Naomi. Maggie was surprised to see Sandra, dressed in a tasteful lavender, seated next to Tara, Zeke's girlfriend, at the back.

As they walked slowly down the aisle, Maggie's eyes were glued on her son and grandson. Little Chloe stood in front of them, still holding tight to the flower girl basket. A moment later, she took her place next to Orson in the front row. It was Brett's idea that Orson served as her escort while he was busy as the best man.

Moments later, Suzan practically floated down the aisle with one arm wrapped in her father's and another in her stepfather's. She took her place in front of the officiant, smiling at Bradley. Within minutes, they were pronounced husband and wife. Maggie fished her linen handkerchief out of her dress pocket, then paused to notice for the first time that Orson had held on to her arm during the entire ceremony.

"Well, it really happened," Brett whispered when he embraced her following the service.

"I know, I can't believe it's over," Maggie said.

"Despite all of the opposition, they finally got married."

"Reminds me of someone else we know."

"Who?" Brett asked, releasing her long enough to search her face.

"It reminds me of us," Maggie said. "The feelings we had for each other in high school, then all of those years of separation and time being married to other people. You had daughters of your own while I raised Bradley. Then, somewhere in the middle of our lives, we found each other again."

"I'm just glad these two are a lot younger and have more time together than we will," Brett said.

"Maybe it's not about the amount of time you have together," Maggie said. "Maybe it's more about the way you spend that time."

***

If you enjoyed To Have And To Holed, check out the next book in the series, Ring Of Deceit, today!

AUTHOR'S NOTE

I'd love to hear your thoughts on my books, the storylines, and anything else that you'd like to comment on—reader feedback is very important to me. My contact information, along with some other helpful links, is listed on the next page. If you'd like to be on my list of "folks to contact" with updates, release and sales notifications, etc.... just shoot me an email and let me know. Thanks for reading!

Also...

... if you're looking for more great reads, Summer Prescott Books publishes several popular series by outstanding Cozy Mystery authors.

CONTACT SUMMER PRESCOTT
BOOKS PUBLISHING

Blog and Book Catalog: http:// summerprescottbooks.com

Email: summer.prescott.cozies@gmail.com

And...be sure to check out the Summer Prescott Cozy Mysteries fan page and Summer Prescott Books Publishing Page on Facebook – let's be friends!

To sign up for our fun and exciting newsletter, which will give you opportunities to win prizes and swag, enter contests, and be the first to know about New Releases, click here: http://summerprescottbook s.com

Printed in Great Britain
by Amazon